The Wandere

A life time of following the Wanderers

by

Robin Prickett

To Trev & Susie

Best wishes

Robin

25TH December 2012

© 2012 Robin Prickett

The right of Robin Prickett to be identified as author of this work has been asserted in accordance with the Copyrights, Designs and Patents Act 1988

ISBN: 978-1-291-04264-1

With thanks to

Like all good stories there are people behind the scenes that need to be thanked, those whose help has enabled me to write this book.

Firstly I would like to thank the football clubs of Wolverhampton and Wycombe Wanderers who have provided me with the cherished memories and subject matter for my book, together with their co-operation in its production.

I need to thank my long suffering wife Linda, although she didn't always agree with my football excursions she does understand my need to make them.

I need to thank my good mate and companion Simon Ivermee who has travelled hundreds of miles with me on our watching of the Wolves, sharing the highs and lows, also being my human sat nav.

Thanks to all at London Wolves for obtaining match tickets and providing travel when I've needed it.

A huge thanks and indebtedness to my son Matthew, whose help with the lap top has been essential, constantly rescuing me when I've pressed the wrong buttons, also daughters Helen and Sarah, together with potential son-in-law Aaron who have also assisted.

Thanks to Neil Jackson, a fellow Wolves supporter whose enthusiastic interest in my book has helped to push me that extra mile.

A big thank you to Christine Stevens who has helped with the proofing and copying together with the sending of numerous emails.

Thanks to Katy Green who has provided the illustrations.

Finally a grateful thanks to everyone connected with the production of this book that has enabled me to realize a dream.

The forward

To the reader,

This is a personal account of my following of two very different football clubs; Wolverhampton and Wycombe Wanderers, although they do have the distinction of being the only two WWFCs in the league. Wolves were one of the original twelve members of the very first football league whilst Wycombe remained non-league until they were promoted to the league in 1993.
I hope you enjoy my recollections as I very much enjoyed writing them.
Robin

CHAPTER ONE

THE EARLY YEARS

When I was growing up in the fifties football wasn't the great TV sport that it is today, match of the day hadn't yet appeared on our screens and most supporters didn't travel miles to watch their favourite team play. The large stadiums were mainly packed with fans local to the area and there wasn't the need to have home and away segregation.

Football was however rapidly becoming a national past time and starting to attract a stronger media attention. When England won the world cup in 1966 fans were being introduced to our beautiful game on a much larger scale than before. It was around this time that my passion for football was being ignited, an interest and pursuit that has grown stronger over the years and still with me today.

As a boy of twelve years old living in the Buckinghamshire town of High Wycombe, I remember that the English professional game consisted, as it is today of 92 clubs, forming a league of four divisions, Divs one and two had twenty two clubs in each division whilst divs three and four were made up of twenty four clubs each respectively. The non- league scene consisted of many smaller leagues with clubs fielding semi-professional and amateur players.
In those days the gulf between professional and non- league football was very apparent and entry into the football league via the fourth division was selective, nowadays due to restructuring and the introduction of automatic promotion the gap has narrowed. My supporting of the "Wanderers" began in the late sixties. Which came first the wolf of Wolverhampton or the swan of Wycombe? Although being born in High Wycombe and spending all my years in the town to date, my first love was that of the wanderers sporting the gold and black strip.

It was probably down to the fact that every Saturday when the football results came on the television the mention of wolves caught my attention, being mad keen on animals, I didn't realise at the time that wolves was also the nickname of Wolverhampton Wanderers football club as well as being the name of some beautiful wild creatures. Thus my love for the club from the West Midlands had begun... Another set of facts unknown to me at the time related to the year 1954, this was the year that Roger Bannister broke the 4 minute mile record, Wolves won their first league division one title and I was born.

Although my heart was with the men from Molineux, being only a teenager I had to spend my early years as a fan following my team's fortunes on the radio and whenever they appeared on the TV. Wolves during this time were undergoing a transitional period and after being one of the most successful English clubs of the fifties were now facing decline, the team that had won the First division three times in that decade had all but gone and the players being brought in to replace the old guard were struggling to cope with the demands of top flight football.

CHAPTER TWO

THE SIXTIES

My beloved Wolves were relegated at the end of the 64/65 season and would play the next two seasons in the second division. It was also around this time that I discovered the other Wanderers in my life, the light and dark blue of Wycombe, my home town team who played their fixtures as an amateur side in the isthmian league. Although both Wanderers were subjected to the same rules of associated football it seemed to me, watching in these early times, that it was a different game that each of them were playing.

I remember attending my first Wycombe game in 1967, a brisk Autumn evening at home to Slough Town in a Mid-week league match, I had travelled to the game from my home by bus with my older cousin, and although this fixture in context would have been considered a minor match, this being my first live football, the memory and excitement has stayed with me forever. Wycombe won the match 1-0 thanks to a Peter Roystone goal but it was the smell of football that had hooked me.

Standing on the open uncovered terrace behind the goal, known affectionately as the gas works end and, then changing at half time to stand behind the other opposite goal referred to as the hospital end, this freedom for supporters to move around the non-seated areas would not be allowed in the professional game.

The aromas that hit the cooling night air consisted of the strong smell of the protective oil that the players rubbed onto their legs to keep warm, the waft of fried onions from the fast food out-let and the scent of pipe and cigarette smoke that encircled the ground. Wycombe at this time were playing their home fixtures at Loakes Park, a ground famous for its fifteen foot sloping pitch, being from the top width to the bottom width.

My first live Wolves game came when I was thirteen, in May 1968 played at the Molineux; the Wolves had gained promotion from the 2nd to the 1st division the season before and were fighting to stay up in the top flight. The opposition that day were Tottenham who themselves needed points at the other end of the table to qualify for Europe. My dad had got us booked on a Tottenham supporter's coach that had been organised by the

Morning Star Public House in High Wycombe and I was the only Wolves fan on board apart from my dad who was neutral.

Arriving at the Molineux for the first time was special and to see the players in the flesh whom I had only seen before in magazines was something else. The stadium was fantastic with masses of gold and black structure cut into a hill with a high south bank terrace, which housed the away support.

On entering the ground I could feel the atmosphere of a place soaked in football history, imagining the great Wolves players that had graced the Molineux pitch in the glory years, and where Europe's top club sides had fallen to the Wanderers under the Wolverhampton flood lights, in the 1950s.

We were in with the away fans, now whether it was because I was a thirteen year old kid or that I cheered for the Wolves in a southern accent I managed to clap them to a 2-1 victory and two vital league points without being harmed. I was lucky to be behind the goal where both Wolves goals were scored, the scorers being Frank Wignall and Derek Parkin, Jimmy Greaves replied for Spurs. I was also privileged to see what had been full back Parkin's first goal for the Wolves and this appearance was one of the 609 that he made for the Wanderers, which remains a club record. Again the experience and the excitement of the occasion will live with me forever.

On the coach journey home I was the only one who was still rejoicing. The Wolves secured Division one status that season and I was relieved that my cheering hadn't been in vain. I had now tasted the euphoria of live football and the thrill and commitment of supporting a football team, except that I was following two, anyone who has read the book or seen the film of Nick Hornby's Fever Pitch will know what I mean.

Bill Shankley, the former Liverpool manager once said "Football was not life and death, it was more important than that", I was firmly hooked and looked forward to my next match. A smoker craves an intake of nicotine in the morning, an alcoholic needs that first drink to start the day, I need a fix of football a la the Wanderers kind to be able focus on life, it's been said that instead of blood flowing through my veins the LIQUID would be called the "dator" i.e. the "liquidator". The liquidator of course was for many years the music played on the public address system at the Molineux before each home game.

As I progressed through my teens both Wanderers enjoyed mixed fortunes and it made interesting watching. As I was still at school during this period most of my watching was of the amateur Wanderers of Wycombe, and I was able to attend most of the home games and quite a lot of their away games. This was possible because Wycombe were members of the isthmian league and most of the competing clubs were from the London area. I well remember booking my seat on coach one bound for grounds; the likes of Enfield, Barking, Sutton and Hendon. Coach one was regarded as the lead vehicle of the away support and mainly used by the younger fans.

CHAPTER THREE

THE SEVENTIES

When we travelled to the London grounds we used to pull up at Shepherd's Bush before the game to have our own kick-around and then after the match had a stop on the return journey for fish and chips. Travelling regularly by coach enabled me to establish a good rapport with fellow supporters and many a lasting friendship developed from my travels. There was one airy scary moment noted when watching Wycombe away at Leytonstone in the early seventies, this was to watch an isthmian league match, when I hadn't journeyed by coach for this game, travelling by train instead. I had gone to the match with three Wycombe friends, one of whom was an avid train spotter and wanted to tour the nearby train depot at Stratford hence the train journey. The tour of the depot had been completed, a good win at Leytonstone had been achieved, but it was on the way home that we had the incident.

We had arrived back at Marylebone station and were waiting for the train to take us home to High Wycombe. We were still draped in our Wycombe colours, scarfs attached to our trousers and sporting blue rosettes. Just then a train pulled in from Oxford carrying hundreds of Millwall "fans" who had just seen their team lose 1-0 at Oxford United. This being the seventies when soccer violence was at its worse and Millwall followers topped the charts in thuggery, a title they are even today reluctant to give up. As the train got slowly closer we could see that every carriage window had been smashed and the train looked like it had returned from a war zone. Then the angry rabble got off the train and started to walk towards us. It was then that my anorak train spotting friend thought it a bright idea to shout out "good old Oxford"; at that point I turned to my other two friends and we agreed, (facing our friend with the warped humour) and telling him "if these approaching morons don't kill you, then we will." As the Millwall procession arrived at where we were standing I could see that they had the typical stereo type appearance of a football hooligan, cropped hair cuts, bovver boots, broken noses, bits missing from their facial features and of course tattoos on tattoos. As we prepared for the possible attack, one of the thugs presumably the leader shouted out "Wycombe who the F...k are they", and walked past, followed by all of his mates. Wycombe were still an amateur club at this point, obviously their name hadn't yet reached the professional world of South East London. We then breathed a big sigh of relief, caught our train home and returned to the peaceful sanity of rural

Buckinghamshire. I recall a bizarre incident at the end of the 74/75 season, relating to the Berks and Bucks final for that campaign. The records show that Thatcham are the holders of the cup, but in fact they had been well BEATEN 4-0 by Wycombe in the FINAL. This quirky fact exists because Wycombe after winning the cup refused to collect it or their winners' medals as a protest towards the Berks and Bucks governing body for their continual refusal of not allowing the Wanderers to participate in the London Senior Cup. The embarrassed Berks and Bucks officials stood red faced as the Wycombe players and club staff headed towards the dressing rooms, walking past the many Wanderers fans who were chanting "We want to play in the London Senior cup"; to this day Wycombe still haven't graced the competition but have honoured and supported the Berks and Bucks cup winning it a record 27 times. Moving into the early to mid-seventies Wycombe were now able to field a very formidable non-league side, including many amateur internationals in their ranks. This also proved to be a very successful time for the club in this period, winning the isthmian league on no fewer than four times and fast gaining respect in the FA cup.

I remember in 1975, having beaten Bournemouth in the 2nd round Wycombe were then drawn at home to Middlesbrough in the 3rd round. Middlesbrough had been enjoying a purple patch in their history and when they were due to play Wycombe in the cup they occupied top spot in the old division one, this being the equivalent to today's Premiership league. The "Borough" were managed by Jack Charlton the former Leeds United star and member of the winning England 1966 world cup final team.

Charlton had put together a resilient and dogged side, sprinkled with senior internationals and the amateurs of Wycombe could expect a tough tie. The game was played out in front of 12,000 fans packed into the Loakes Park ground and on the pitch Wycombe more than matched their professional opponents. The game ended 0-0 with Wycombe having the best chance of the match when a headed attempt by Alan Phillips, the Wanderers captain and centre half flew narrowly passed the post, five minutes from time.

After the match Jack Charlton, referring to Wycombe's performance said "You played well but when we get you back to our place and without your famous slope were Gunnar murder yer ". In the replay Wycombe were "murdered "1-0 by an 89th minute David Armstrong goal.

The amateurs of Wycombe had given their professional hosts one heck of a scare and had earn the greatest of respect. When the final whistle went a minute later the WHOLE of the stadium erupted with the relieved home fans joining the away fans in a chorus of "WYCOMBE...WYCOMBE ...WYCOMBE," the Middlesbrough team formed a tunnel of honour and applauded the gallant Wycombe players off the pitch. The attendance at Middlesbrough that evening was over 30,000, and was only bettered once that season by the visit of Manchester United; it was good to be a Wycombe fan that night.

Wolves during the seventies had mixed fortunes; having regained first division status the club produced some notable performances. Still in my teens I was dependant on lifts to the Molineux and so my visits at this point were restricted to a few games each season thus relying largely on the TV and radio to keep me in touch with the latest news on the Wanderers. One game which I'm glad was televised, particularly as I was unable to get to see it live was the 71/72 Division One home fixture against Arsenal. The game took place in wintry conditions and I recall that Arsenal led 1-0 at half time. The second half was played in a snow blizzard but the Wanderers turned in a five goal performance, running out 5-1 winners, one of the goals, scored by Dave Wagstaffe was voted Match of The Day's goal of the month.

Wolves had also returned to European football that season and had enjoyed success in the U.E.F.A cup, reaching an all-England final against

Tottenham. The final was contested over two legs. Unfortunately for Wolves and me we lost the first leg at Molineux 1-2 and despite a spirited 1-1 second leg draw at Tottenham we were beaten 2-3 on aggregate, again we had a gem of a goal to savour from Dave Wagstaffe in the away leg, he didn't score many but when he did they were usually belters.

The following 72/73 season Wolves maintained their fine form finishing 5th in the league and again qualifying for the following seasons U.E.F.A cup. Also Wolves were to achieve success in the League cup; I remember travelling with a friend to the Molineux for a third round tie against Sheffield Wednesday. The game kicked off at 7-45 and my memories from that game were how bright the Sheffield Wednesday kit was glowing under the Molineux floodlights, thankfully that was the brightest thing about their performance as Wolves ran out comfortable 3-1 winners.

Only downer on the trip was that we had travelled from High Wycombe to Wolverhampton by train via London and could only get back as far as London before the network closed down for the night.

This meant a very cold few hours spent in Marylebone station until the service resumed again in the morning, all part of being a devoted supporter. Wolves managed further progress in the competition, in fact reaching the two legged semi-final where Tottenham Hotspur were to again provide the opposition. Unfortunately just as in the first leg of the U.E.F.A cup final Tottenham left Molineux with a 2-1 victory.

Wolves once again responded giving another heroic display in the away second leg, with the clock ticking down were drawing the game 1-1 but 2-3 behind on aggregate when star striker John Richards scored making it 2-1 to Wolves on the night, levelling the tie 3-3 on aggregate, and taking the game into extra time. Then Alan Gilzean scored a goal during the extra 30 minutes putting the Spurs 4-3 up and through to the final, breaking our hearts once again.

Wolves continued the bride's maid theme by also reaching the semi-final of the FA cup. Having negotiated the first four rounds of the competition without conceding a goal then lost to Leeds by the only goal of the game. The 73/74 season saw Wolves temporally lose the bride's maid tag reaching the league cup final against hot favourites Manchester City. The city side had wall to wall quality with the likes of Colin Bell, Rodney Marsh, Denis Law etc., but the Wolves having not won a major trophy since beating Blackburn Rovers 3-0 in the 1960 FA cup final had a deep hunger and desire to overcome the city slickers. Wolves had their own stars that day, goal keeper Gary Pierce was to play his finest game in a Wolves shirt and the brilliant John Richards turned in another fantastic display scoring the winning goal in a 2-1 Wanderers win.

Richards was at the peak of his career and had formed a deadly strike partnership with Derek "the doog "Dougan; and now regularly finished Wolves top goal scorer plundering goals in all the competitions that he played in; it seemed the only person in the land who didn't appreciate John's talent was the ENGLAND national team manager. The 74/75 season saw Wolves occupy a mid-table league position and two games that stand out in my mind were the 7-1 home win against Chelsea and the 0-0 draw at Newcastle.

The thrashing of Chelsea was the biggest home win for many years and the goal feast was indeed a game to cherish but the game at Newcastle had other memorable qualities. Although a mid-week fixture I and a friend managed to make the long trip to Newcastle. We travelled by train to the cold North east, this being my first visit to this part of the world since my trip to Middlesbrough earlier in the year for the Wycombe cup match. My friend was a Newcastle fan but had left the area and moved south some 25 years after his 5th birthday and hadn't been back since. We arrived at the St. James Park just before kick- off and were greeted by a piercing glow from the floodlights. As this was during the days when you could pay at the turnstiles on the day of the match we headed for the nearest entrance. On entering the ground I recall the many steps that we had to climb to get to the level where we were standing.

We soon realised that we had inadvertently chosen the "toon" end, where all the diehard home fans were gathered, everywhere there was masses of black and white with scarfs held aloft. Chants of "super mac" were ringing out all around us .NB. The name Supermac, referred to Malcolm MacDonald who was the Geordies local hero at the time.

Luckily we weren't wearing any colours and managed somehow to mingle with one of the most partisan football crowds in the country without being detected. The atmosphere was very intimidating with the home supporters baying for a Newcastle goal that would send the whole place into raptures. Wave after wave of Newcastle attacks like a black and white tide were repeatedly thwarted by the Wolves rear guard defending in depth, at times resembling a scene from the battle of the Alamo, I'm sure Davy Crockett had lined up beside Frank Munro that evening to keep the marauders out. Wolves although battered held on to a valuable 0-0 draw. That performance still remains as one of the best defensive displays that I've seen from a Wolves back four, keeping a clean sheet and collecting a valuable away point against a very good Newcastle side.

After recovering from watching 90 minutes of dogged resistance we set about our journey home getting as far as Euston station before the railway network shut down, thus spending another night waiting for the first morning train back home. The 75/76 season was a shock to the system, having enjoyed a good start to the 70s decade Wolves finished 20th in the division and therefore occupied the 3rd relegation place returning back to the second division. The 76/77 season kicked-off with Wolves having retained most of the players that went down from the 75/76 campaign. Having this strong squad enabled Wolves to produce a serious promotion challenge right from the start of the season. The season went right down to the wire with Wolves and Chelsea fighting for the honour to be top dogs. When the sides met at Molineux towards the end of the season, a John Richards goal for Wolves in a 1-1 draw was enough to see them return as champions and Chelsea secured the runners up spot.

Into the 77/78 season and a time for consolidation after promotion, finishing a creditable 15th in the league and retaining first division status. One game that springs to mind was the 4th round FA cup tie at Arsenal. Once again entry was payable on the day and once again I ended up in the wrong end, behind the goal with all the Arsenal hard core in. Arsenal took the lead through ex wanderer Alan Sunderland early in the game and there were celebrations all around me, I forced a strained smile and imagined he was still wearing a Wolves shirt not wishing to reveal my true feelings as I was surrounded by Arsenal fans.

Wolves battled back and drew level through a wonder strike from Kenny Hibbitt, this time the smile wasn't forced although I had to curb my jubilations. Wolves had clawed their way back into the game and with centre half Bob Hazell majestic in defence things were looking more comfortable. Hazell had been keeping Arsenal striker Malcolm "super mac" MacDonald, their expensive signing from Newcastle very quiet, shadowing him everywhere; then disaster struck, literally, Graham Rix, the Arsenal mid-fielder who had been irritating and had shown bouts of petulance all afternoon tangled with Hazell, causing the big defender to lose his cool.

There then followed a huge right hook that Frank Bruno would have been proud of, despatched by Hazell, landing firmly on the chin of Rix, laying the agitator out cold. Unfortunately the referee didn't share the view that Rix had received his just rewards and Wolves were promptly reduced to ten men. To add insult to injury the departure of Bob Hazell allowed Macdonald to escape his shackles giving him more freedom of movement and he netted a late goal to send Arsenal through 2-1 winners. The 78/79 season Wolves finished 18th in the league and again reached the semi-final of the FA cup losing out again 2-0 to Arsenal, I'm getting sick of being beaten by North London clubs in major cup competitions.

To close the seventies decade Wolves signed off in great style, a 6th placing in the league and another visit to Wembley to contest the 79/80

League Cup final where Nottingham Forest were the opposition. Forest had won this cup for the past two seasons but a solitary goal by the determined Wolves prevented them making it a hat trick of wins; the goal scorer was Andy Gray who at one point was the most expensive footballer in Britain when he signed for Wolves from Aston Villa in September 1979 for 1.5 million pounds, the record had replaced the earlier one set when Steve Daley had been transferred by Wolves to Manchester City for 1.4 million pounds in the same transaction.

Captain of the Wolves that day was Emlyn Hughes who after spending many years as a Liverpool player had a short Wolves career where he picked up the only domestic medal that had previously eluded him, a League Cup medal.

CHAPTER FOUR

THE EIGHTIES

Then game the eighties which Wolves started with optimism, the 80/81 saw a position of 18th in the league obtained and another FA cup semi- final reached. Once again the opposition were from North London in the familiar guise of Tottenham. Wolves and Tottenham fought out a 2-2 draw but the replay went the way of Tottenham again, running out 3-0 winners. The 81/82 season saw Wolves latest stay in the top division come to an abrupt end, finishing 21st in the table and confirming 2nd division football for the following season. To accompany relegation the club went into administration as the financial pressures increased. The club eventually came out of administration but was far from stable. As I progressed through my early adult years I was able to attend more matches and still tried to get to the Molineux as much as possible, also attending the games when the Wolves played in London. It was when going to watch the Wolves in the capital that I experienced my first "aggro" although not on the pitch or even on the terraces.

The occasion in question happened during the 82/83 season when the Wolves were playing Fulham at Craven Cottage on New Year's day, in a second division fixture; I'm now in my twenties and single, so myself and a friend called Colin thought it would be a good idea to book into a B&B in Hammersmith and celebrate new year's eve at the Hammersmith Palais then off to the footie the next day.

The first part of the plan was fine and we had managed to get booked in at a B&B but because it was full we couldn't get into the Palais. We then decided to sample the hospitality of the local pubs in the area and stumbled across what seemed a friendly establishment playing good Irish folk music. We joined a party of Irish revellers and decided to see in the New Year, in their company.

The hours passed quickly and several drinks later we were approaching 12pm and in high spirits. Unfortunately just into the New Year the mood changed dramatically as appearing on our table was a large hat being used to collect donations to help fund the IRA cause. Now the troubles in Ireland had been going on for some years but this was England and we weren't expecting what had been a pleasant evening to end this way. Those who had been sharing a laugh and a drink with us were now giving us menacing looks; it didn't help when my mate told them where they could stick their hat. Needless to say we didn't make any contributions but made a hasty exit and retired to our B&B, stopping briefly at a late night burger bar.

The next day was much more civilised and the Wolves secured a fine 3-1 away win. For the remainder of the eighties Wolves failed to paper over the cracks of their financial difficulties and problems on and off the pitch resurfaced causing the club to spiral towards the basement league. Despite one brief season back in the top flight, the once famous Wanderers now found themselves in the 4th division trying to avoid the drop to the Conference league. The club were relegated from the old first division in season 83/84 to division four by season 86/87, this all happened in consecutive seasons. With the club facing winding up orders, the stadium half closed, needing repairs the future looked very uncertain.

It was probably the lowest point in time of my supporting the Wolves, and to watch my club dying before my eyes was like a bad dream. Attendances for league matches had dropped to 5000 and under, and during the 86/87 season the club recorded probably the worst FA cup result in its illustrious history, having failed to beat non- league Chorley after two 1-1 draws then lost at the THIRD attempt crashing out of the competition 0-3.

The Wolves motto is "out of darkness cometh light," between the years 1983 to 1987 the Molineux was certainly in darkness, then cometh the light. Just in time a rescue package was put together, headed by Sir Jack Hayward. Graham Turner was installed as manager who signed Steve Bull from neighbours West Brom for a fee of around £50,000. Bull was to become the Wolves all-time top goal scorer and modern day legend, scoring no less than 306 goals in his Wolverhampton career, a club record. The combination helped stop the slide that had seen the Wanderers plummet through the divisions and a recovery plan was quickly installed, including the restoration of a decaying Molineux.

Thankfully the revival was as swift as the decline and the new look Wolves having now stabilised, aided by the financial backing of chairman Jack Hayward progressed back through the divisions. The 86/87 season turned around and the Wolves at last were heading back up the table, finishing in 4th position; unfortunately narrowly missing out to Aldershot in the play-offs. The 87/88 season the Wolves made no mistake winning the division and starting the long way back also securing the Sherpa Van Trophy with a 2-0 win against Burnley at Wembley. Wycombe had now obtained promotion from the isthmian league into the Conference and had now taken on a semi- professional status. The Conference league could be described as the un-official division five as the winners are promoted to the fourth division of the Football league. My most frustrating time happened during the 88/89 season when Wolves had a morning kick off for a division two fixture at Bury and Wycombe had a 3pm conference start at Chorley, just a few miles further up the road. A group of us decided to do the double header. First point of call was at Bury where Wolves crashed 3-1 despite a Floyd Street goal then on to Chorley. Wycombe raced to a 2-0 lead and were heading for a comfortable away win until Kevin Day their centre half was sent off and the Wanderers slipped to a 3-2 defeat. The summary of the day played two, lost two, scored 3, conceded 6, nil points and a fruitless 500 mile round trip.

CHAPTER FIVE

THE NINETIES

The start to the 90/91 season produced an interesting incident; Wolves were playing away at Oldham which is usually a tough venue to get a result. What we didn't need that day was a finicky referee, but of course we got one. Stevie Bull had put in another battling performance scoring twice and then getting sent off for a "hand bag" clash with an Oldham defender, who would have thought that his job was done getting rid of Bully; ten men Wolves lost the game 2-3. The one amusing part of the day happened at half time, now for many years the music played at Wolves home games as the teams came on to the pitch was a reggae instrumental called "the liquidator" by Harry J and the All-stars. As with most tunes played regularly over the tannoy system it doesn't take long before the fans convert them into football chants, this one was no exception. The main content was aimed at our lovely local rivals West Brom. The basic chorus went "come on you Wolves, F..K off West Brom; now after several years of practice the fans had it to perfection. It was then on police advice that our liquidator was replaced as it was now considered to be offensive and provocative. The West Brom song was therefore retired and put to rest with the original 70s vinyl record seemingly gone but not forgotten. Here in Oldham I found that I was in a time warp where the modern civilisation hadn't quite reached this part of the world yet, standing on an antiquated terrace behind a goal in the quaint ground of Oldham football club. The ground itself is situated in a very residential area, homely houses with pretty flower beds and a strong communal bonding. I'm not sure if when they started playing music for the half time entertainment, if the announcer started with "hi boys and girls". Then it happened over the tannoy came our old friend, the liquidator, it seemed it hadn't been away when the 3000 travelling Wolves fans quickly found voice "come on you Wolves etc." After a couple of minutes of air play there was a loud scratching sound as the stylus was roughly pushed off the record, followed by "I think we've had enough of that one thank you"; and normal service resumed.

It was also during the 90/91 season that I experienced that the same thing can also be different. Wolves were playing Bristol Rovers away in a division two fixture and because the Rovers were having their ground re-developed they were using Conference club Bath City's ground for their home fixtures. I had travelled to Bath to watch the game by car with my friend Simon and as we neared the stadium we found that the Police had closed many of the approach roads, so we had to park up about a mile from the ground and complete our journey on foot. As we arrived at the ground we were greeted by a heavy Police presence, they even had a helicopter in the air. The club bar was for home fans only and strictly out of bounds to away supporters. On reaching the turnstiles we were frisked and then shepherded to a particular part of the ground where we had to remain for the duration of the game. There was also heavy segregation in place, in the form of wire fencing plus many lines of police and stewards. The atmosphere was quite hostile, purely down to the enforcements and restrictions imposed. The actual match which Wolves drew 1-1 was played without any serious incident. Ten days later I returned to Bath, this being a Tuesday night and Bath City were playing Wycombe in a Conference league match. I had travelled this time to the game on a supporters coach. When the coach arrived it parked outside the main entrance to the ground and we got off and went straight to the Bath supporters bar, where we were welcomed in and enjoyed a drink and chat with some of the home fans. Suitably refreshed we left the bar and entered the ground, taking up our position, standing behind one of the goals. As was our normal practice when watching Wycombe we faced the pitch behind the goal that our forwards were attacking. When half time came we changed ends and stood behind the other goal passing through the Bath fans, some heading the other way. Wycombe won the match 2-1 and we re-boarded our coach and left for home. Within just TEN days I was left with the feeling how a same place could be so different.

CHAPTER SIX

INTERESTING SITUATIONS

Supporting the Wanderers has certainly led to some interesting situations, like the time I went to watch Wycombe play at Macclesfield in the Conference. I had travelled by train to the match with some friends and we had a fifteen minute walk to the ground from the railway station. The game itself finished eight minutes late which meant that we had to move quickly if we were going to catch our train for home on time.

On leaving the ground a friendly policeman realizing our situation came to our rescue. He said there was a small gang of hooligans waiting around the corner ready to cause trouble and that it would be quicker and safer if he gave us a lift to the railway station in his Black Maria, so we piled in the back of his vehicle. When we passed the yobs they were cheering and waving their hands, being too thick to understand that we hadn't been arrested, just hitching a ride, my only time in the back of a police van, honest guv.

How many fans can say that they saw their FOOTBALL team play a league fixture at a test CRICKET GROUND? I remember December 1972 when Corinthian Casuals found themselves without a place to play their home games so they played Wycombe at The Oval, the headquarters of Surrey County Cricket and one of the venues used by England for test matches. It was very strange to see the Oval partially roped off and being used to accommodate football.

Then there was the time we followed the Wolves to Barnsley, again my Wolves chum Simon was on board together with a friend called Ron who is a Barnsley fan and season ticket holder. We travelled by car and arrived at Barnsley in good time. Ron had his season ticket and we had tickets for seats in the away stand. As Ron is an exiled tyke, back in his native town for a few hours and a regular attendee at the Oakwell stadium we asked him where the best place for us to park was.

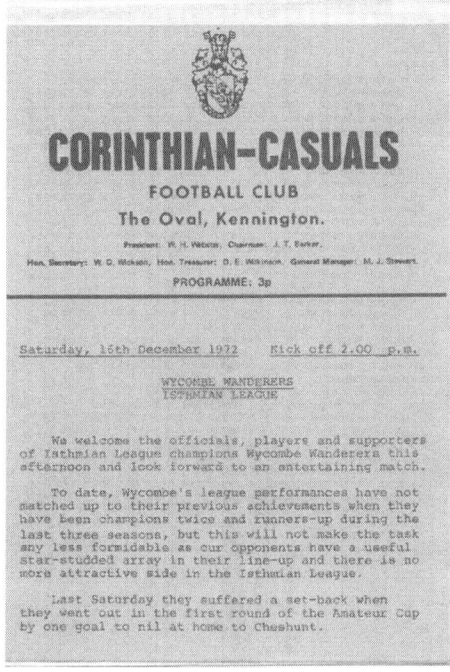

He promptly directed us to a large car park that was designated for away fans only. We agreed to meet back at the car after the game, wishing Ron well and telling him that we hoped that his team would lose. The game went well for us and Wolves won 2-1. Simon and I returned to the car feeling well pleased but no sign of Ron. After about 25 minutes a disgruntled Ron turned up. As he reached us he said, his voice having returned to its original broad Yorkshire accent and Ron looking like a double for Victor Meldrew from One foot in the grave; "Bloody Coppers, they wouldn't let me through, they said that I can't enter car park till ALL them Wolves fans ad gone" Ron further added "I ope they all aven't left, two of them are giving me lift ome," we had quite a chuckle on the journey back.

One game that sticks out in my memory took place in 1984 at Loakes Park. The match was between Wycombe and Leicester City and was played because both clubs were founded in 1884, and this game was part of both clubs centenary celebrations. Wycombe were still a non-league side during this period and faced the full first team of division one Leicester, including a young Gary Lineker. Although the match ended 0-0 with the honours all square it proved to be of an entertaining and competitive nature. As we further progressed through the nineties this decade proved to be a very historic and emotional period of my watching of the Wanderers.

Wycombe after many years of playing their home games at Loakes Park moved to a new ground just a few miles from the old ground. They named the new stadium Adams Park in honour of Frank Adams, a former player and patron who had previously given the deeds of Loakes Park to the Wanderers. Wycombe were now under the managerial guidance of Martin O'Neil and he and the club were preparing the Wanderers for an assault on the Conference that would earn them promotion to the football league.

CHAPTER SEVEN

MORE NINETIES

Martin O'Neil was to be invaluable to Wycombe bringing a wealth of experience to the club but his biggest asset was his characteristic enthusiasm which manifested in his teams performances. The 91/92 campaign was one of if not the best in Conference history, with Wycombe and Colchester going neck and neck for the title. At the end of the season both clubs finished joint 1st with 94 points which was 21 points clear of Kettering in 3rd place and a new Conference record for the number of points achieved by any club in a season. Unfortunately Colchester had a superior goal difference to that of Wycombe and were promoted; this was partly due to the head to head matches between the two sides. When the teams had earlier met at Layer Road Colchester, the home side ran out 3-0 victors, but it was the game at Adams Park Wycombe that had a major and dramatic impact in deciding where the title and spoils were heading. The game was poised at 1-1 and deep into injury time when Scott Barrett, the Colchester goal keeper made a huge drop kick up field, with wind assistance the ball sailed over a stunned Paul Hyde in the Wycombe goal giving Colchester a 2-1 win. What was also so annoying for me, the unlikely goal scorer, goalie Scott Barrett was previously a Wolves youngster. The next season 92/93 Wycombe made sure and finished a clear top on 83 points, 15points clear of 2nd place Bromsgrove Rovers. Wycombe were now a top non- league side and it came as little surprise when they won the FA Trophy in 1993 which was only surpassed by the winning of the Conference in the same season and thus earning promotion to the football league. I remember saying to friends it doesn't matter who or where but I have to see Wycombe's first match in the football league.

When the 93/94 fixtures came out, it just had to be CARLISLE UTD away! Still it had to be done and what a great day out it was we were so close to Scotland I'm sure that I heard the bag pipes playing in the back ground. Wycombe started their football league career with a 2-2 draw in this fixture at Carlisle.

Their first ever goal in the league was scored for them, courtesy of an opponent, but their second goal which secured their first Football League point was scored by Steve Guppy, who later in his career would earn an England International call up at senior level. Wycombe took their excellent non- league form into the Football League and were rapidly consolidating their position in the division, proving to be a hard team to beat.

Their progress was such that they managed to reach the two legged area final of the Auto Glass Trophy against Swansea. This tie also served as a handy learning curve for the club. Wycombe narrowly lost the first leg in Swansea 3-1 and had it all to do in the second leg if they were to reach the national final. Wycombe's opponents Swansea, who at the time were experiencing financial difficulties and had done well themselves to reach this stage of the competition, and with the possibility of a lucrative Wembley final it had helped to toughen their resilience.

The evening of the second leg proved to be very interesting, Wycombe being novice hosts at this level of entertaining seemed very unprepared. The new Adams Park, ground staff and stewards had been used to the non-league scene and had little exposure to the ugly side of the professional game. Swansea's usual away support in the current climate was very moderate but for the Wycombe cup match it had swelled considerably. The away end was surging with the many Swansea "fans" quite a few had tagged on with the regulars because it was a cup tie and the added opportunity for the hooligan element to mingle within the large crowd.

The atmosphere in the stadium was very highly charged and there was an uneasy feeling that something non-football was going to happen. The Adams Park ground had been built in keeping with Wycombe as being a family orientated club and the whole set up had been designed for comfort and not so much attention placed on crowd restriction. Then it happened, just before kick-off, a few idiots at first from the stand housing the away support stepped over the safety barriers and brushed past the handful of stewards racing onto the pitch. Then a larger number of "fans" seized the opportunity and joined the morons already running amok, some parading

Welsh banners under the misapprehension that they were representing their country.

The angry mob then ran the length of the pitch to the opposite end where the home fans were standing and tried to goad them into some response. The Wycombe faithful just stared in disbelief at the hooligans, offering them no form of retaliation. After what seemed an age the marauding mob then returned frustrated to the away enclosure where the bemused stewards shepherded them to their seats.

A small police presence THEN formed a line in front of the Swansea fans allowing the game to start. Following the earlier drama Wycombe failed in their attempts to retrieve the tie despite winning the second leg 1-0 and Swansea went through 3-2 on aggregate to the Wembley final. The irony of this story was that Swansea shortly returned to Wycombe for a league fixture. This time the genuine Swansea fans that turned up were greeted by a heavy police presence, with trained dogs and a hovering helicopter in the air. Inside the ground was an army of vigilant stewards and more police, the problem was only about a hundred visitors had made the journey, making it two cases of miscommunication? Recalling at this time was also a disaster in the 94/95 FA cup for Wolves. They had previously earned a creditable 1-1 draw at Crystal Palace and we had optimism for a result in the replay. Unfortunately on the night Wolves again showed defensive frailties in front of the home Faithfull and lost 1-4. It didn't help when on the way home; having travelled about five of the one hundred and twelve miles of the journey my car breaks down.

Being in the AA I managed to get road side help and a chatty mechanic came to our assistance. Whilst he was inspecting the car he was talking to us in a broad west midlands brogue. He noticed that we had southern accents and asked had we been to the match. When we said that we had he said that we must be pleased with the result, presuming that we were Palace supporters. When we said that we were Wolves fans, a wide smile spread across his face and he said that he had THREE things to say to us; FIRSTLY that he couldn't fix the car and that he would have to ring his mate who would tow us home; SECONDLY that he was a West Brom fan and THIRDLY his mate was also a West Brom fan.

The situation just got worse; I wish that we had said that we were Palace fans for a few hours, West Brom being arch rivals of the Wolves.

Wolves meanwhile had maintained a steady improvement in the league and the many goals of Steve Bull had helped return the Wanderers to the second tier. The strong financial backing of Chairman Sir Jack Hayward was having a positive effect on the club and the re-development of the Molineux stadium had commenced. On the playing side the squad were preparing for an assault that hopefully would see premiership football in the near future at Wolverhampton. The 94/95 season looked if the dream of returning to the elite was on. Wolves finished 4th in the league and played Bolton in the two legged play-off semi-final. Despite dominating the 1st leg at Molineux and creating numerous chances they only won 2-1 and the 2nd leg at Bolton was always going to be difficult and so it proved. Bolton won the leg 1-0 taking the match into extra time; they scored a second in the added thirty minutes sending them through 3-2 on aggregate, another season that promised so much ending on a flat note.

    It wasn't long however before the Wolves were again knocking on the Premiership door, the 96/97 season saw the Wanderers finish in 3rd spot in the league and another chance via the play offs. The team standing in the Wanderers way of a Wembley final was Crystal Palace who had finished 6th in the league. The first leg at Crystal Palace went horribly wrong, in what had been an evenly contested match the Wanderers conceded late goals to end up losing 1-3 and thus making an uphill challenge for the second leg. The second leg started well with Wolves well on top and deservingly taking the lead.

    Unfortunately Palace equalized against the run of play and the Wanderers again trailed by two goals on aggregate. Wolves did find the net for a second time but Palace held out for a 2-1 defeat and went through 4-3 on aggregate, another missed opportunity. There was one highlight of the 96/97 season the league double over rivals West Brom. I was fortunate to see both matches, starting with the 4-2 away win at the Hawthorns, where striker Ewan Roberts netted a hat trick and earned a place in the Wanderers hall of fame.

    The match at Molineux went the way of Wolves 2-0. The 97/98 season saw the Wolves obtain a position of 9th in the league and reach another FA cup semi-final. The opposition was Arsenal and the venue Villa Park. I remember battling with the heavy congested traffic on the M6 motorway, then parking the car, a quick sprint to the ground, through the turnstiles, up the steps to my seat just in time to see Arsenal score the only goal of the game.

    It was during Wycombe's seventh season in the Football League that the moment I had been both looking forward to and dreading occurred. Wycombe had been drawn to play Wolves in the 2nd round of the 1999/2000 league cup, the tie to be played over two legs. This was the first time that the paths of my two favourite clubs had crossed. The first leg was at Wycombe and I obviously had mixed feelings. On the evening of the first leg, walking into the Adams Park stadium, a Wycombe friend of mine, knowing that I followed both clubs asked me who I was supporting that night. I replied "the Wanderers of course", the friend said "I thought so" and as he walked on I could see by the change of facial expression that the penny had dropped as he eventually realized both teams are wanderers.

The match itself had few chances but the Wolves managed to take a 1-0 lead back to Molineux thanks to a Keith Curle penalty scored midway through the second half. I remember to mark my special occasion the official Wycombe photographer took pictures of myself posing with two of the Wolves stars Steve Sedgley and Neil Emblem respectively, I also had a match programme signed by both sets of players which has pride and place in my vast collection of Wolves and Wycombe programmes.

The second leg at the Molineux proved to be a very testing time for me, Wolves with their 1-0 lead from the first leg embarked on a defensive suicide and gifted Wycombe the perfect start by scoring an own goal, thus squaring the tie. Mayhem soon spread through the rest of the Wolves team and a spirited Wycombe soon grabbed the initiative. Wycombe went on to win 4-2 and the tie 4-3. This I found very strange, where I would have normally cheered Wycombe's performance I found the ease that they had dismissed Wolves to be embarrassing, leaving me with mixed emotions.

Then to further add to coincidence, later in that season Wolves youth were drawn to play Wycombe youth in the Alliance cup played at High Wycombe. As I only lived a short distance from the venue I was easily able to view the potential stars of both clubs without having to travel far. In the Wolves line up that day, at centre forward was the highly rated Colin Larkin who had scored his only Wolves goal at senior level against Wycombe in the 2nd leg of the 2-4 league cup defeat. Playing centre half in the Wycombe side was Roger Johnson whose job was to mark Larkin. Wolves won the game 3-2 and Larkin scored a hat trick. Now the irony of the story is that the guy who scored three goals is currently plying his trade at division one side Hartlepool United and the player who was marking him has now joined the Wolves via Wycombe, Cardiff and Birmingham for a club record transfer fee in the region of 7 million pounds. Also during the season of this cup match, myself and wife at the time were acting as hosts for young Wycombe players who were staying away from home and needed accommodation. I remember that Roger Johnson who had joined Wycombe from Bournemouth was still settling into the area and so spent a couple of nights with us whilst he was sorting himself out, and I now say to our youngest daughter that she once had a 7 million pound footballer staying in her bedroom.

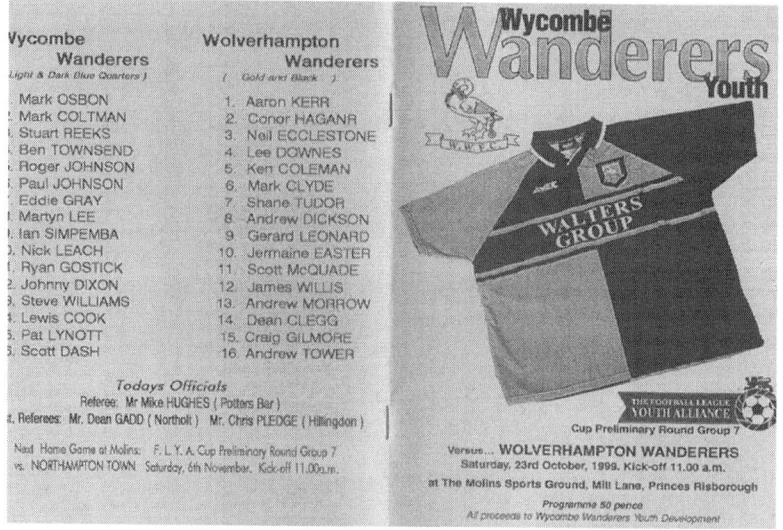

There have been many memorable moments in my Wanderers watching, some I try to forget but most are little gems stored in my memory banks and are recalled on occasions for when I have travelled hundreds of miles in cold and dark conditions to watch a game when the lads have not performed to the full extent of their abilities and I have asked myself, "what am I doing here"; as a supporter all I expect is that the players give their 100% as those that follow them do.

One little gem happened in my first away derby at West Brom, the season was 1989/1990. The game didn't start out to well for the Wolves, with the Albion taking the lead in the first half and grabbing the early bragging rights, much to the delight of the fans wearing the Tesco carrier bags. The Wanderers had in their side that day three ex-"baggies", Andy Thompson, Robbie Dennison and the one and only Steve Bull. During the game "Bully" was subjected to the predictable taunts from the Albion fans of "bull shit, bull shit" etc., which of course was their way of saying "wish you hadn't left us Steve".

Later in the game a Robbie Dennison free kick got the Wolves a deserved equaliser which quietened down the home support and when Bully scored in the 90th minute myself and the rest of the travelling fans shared in his retribution and obvious delight.

One of the most dramatic Wolves matches in recent years took place in the championship at Bristol City; there was drama even before the match and certainly halfway through the game. The results for season 1998/1999 had been inconsistent and after the defeat at Ipswich the Wolves board felt that manager Mark McGee should be relieved of his duties and that his then assistant Colin Lee should be made caretaker manager.

Lee's first game in charge was Bristol City away. The game started like many that season when Bristol took the lead and we were again chasing the game but what we weren't expecting was the Wanderers to respond with SIX goals of their own without further reply, thus winning the match 6-1. Even more frustrating for the sacked Mark McGee was that the striker HE signed at the beginning of the season, David Connolly who hadn't scored a goal in Wolves colours, up to this point nets FOUR times. This fixture had everything including the unrehearsed "entertainment" at halftime. Most clubs now have a mascot, i.e. somebody dressed up in usually a ridiculous costume parading around the pitch before and at halftime of a match. We have at Wolves the tasteful "Wolfe". Bristol City has a black cat as theirs. To add to the line-up that day, one of the sponsors for Bristol City provided three mascots dressed as pigs to help promote their products. When halftime arrived all FIVE mascots had congregated by the entrance to the pitch where the public address was being conducted.

The next thing that happened appeared to be a scuffle breaking out amongst the mascots, and what seemed initially as friendly banter was now undertaking a more serious situation; although it was hard not to laugh at the sight of Wolfe chasing after the three pigs. The crowd naturally encouraged the delinquent mascots which were eventually brought under control by several red faced stewards.

The papers the next day were full of the modern day version of "the three little pigs and the big bad wolf".

CHAPTER EIGHT

THE NAUHTIES

Starting the decade of the naughties, Wycombe were to achieve their finest FA cup run to date. In season 2000/2001 the ambitious Martin O'Neil had now left to manage premiership side Aston Villa, leaving behind a club fast finding its feet in the professional game.

The Wanderers of Wycombe were now under the guidance of Laurie Sanchez who with his players embarked on a remarkable cup run. Having safely negotiated the 1st and 2nd rounds Wycombe were drawn at home to Grimsby Town in round three. Wycombe had never previously progressed past this round and despite some past heroic efforts hadn't even SCORED a goal at this stage of the competition. Their opponents in Grimsby would give them the opportunity to advance into unknown territory.

Grimsby was known as a tough home side but not so fearsome on their travels. The tie was set, the fans were ready but Grimsby hadn't read the script and took the lead, now we had to score. The Grimsby defence stood defiant against a constant barrage of Wycombe attacks all through the game but was only finally bridged late in the second half when defender Paul McCarthy scored the equalizer and earned his side a replay. I remember going to the replay on a supporters coach. This being a cold January night, snow on the ground, every other fixture cancelled due to the bad weather and we were heading to Grimsby bordered by the cold North Sea.

The first thing that we did when we got off the coach in Grimsby was to sample the famous local fish & chips. My piece of cod was so large that it filled the plate, I'm sure that its tail was still flapping, it was so fresh... That was a good start to the evening. We then entered the ground expecting a tough time. Now it could have been the cold northern air or the sheer determination of the boys in blue because Wycombe were outstanding, racing to a 3-0 lead and although Grimsby pulled a goal back, Wycombe held on for a notable win and a place in the fourth round draw.

At this stage in the 3rd round Wolves were playing on the Sunday at Nottingham Forest, being manager Dave Jones first game in charge of the Wanderers. Wolves won a tense game 1-0 thanks to a late second half goal from Adam Proudlock. On the way home from Nottingham myself and friend Simon were listening to the fourth round draw on the radio and once again, in a short space of time, out of the bag came Wycombe Wanderers will play at home to Wolverhampton Wanderers.

Those few words broad cast on the air waves created havoc with my brain cells, I turned to Simon and we both said "No", nearly causing us to have a crash on the motor way, luckily the car was on auto pilot and we managed to get home safely. This of course, unlike the two legs of the league cup when the two met earlier would be played as one match, unless a replay was required. The match was played at a snow covered Adams Park and was an evenly contested tie. Andy Rammel fired Wycombe ahead in the first half only for Carl Robinson to equalize midway through the second. The tie was heading for a replay when Wycombe's on loan striker from Chelsea Sam Parkin crashed home what proved to be the winner.

Once again the Wanderers in light and dark blue had triumphed against the Wanderers in gold and black. Wycombe's reward in the next round was a home tie against Wimbledon. This tie was to be a thorough examination of Wycombe's character and resolve as the match was going away from them when Wimbledon stormed to a 2-0 lead. However Wycombe clawed their way back and managed a 2-2 draw.

The replay was also incident packed, Wimbledon scored in the 1st minute from kick off and Wycombe who were already fielding an injury ravaged side suffered a further set back when striker Andy Rammel had to be replaced after receiving a further knock. Wycombe however settled to the uphill task and managed to equalize later in the half through Dave Carroll. The tie remained even well into the second period but took a further twist when Wycombe went down to ten men, due to Michael Simpson being red carded. As the game headed into the last minute Wimbledon were awarded a penalty.

Despair however was turned to delight when Martin Taylor in the Wycombe goal pulled off a tremendous save; the tie again ended all square, resulting in extra time. In keeping with the earlier drama, Wimbledon AGAIN took the lead in the first minute of extra time; surely this was the end of ten men Wycombe's resistance but Paul McCarthy, the Wycombe centre half had other ideas and levelled the scores in the last minute of extra time forcing a penalty shoot-out, consisting of five kicks, for each side. Wycombe this time grabbed the initiative scoring the first penalty whilst Wimbledon missed theirs and were now behind for the first time in the match, the next two penalties were both despatched and Wycombe led 2-1. The third penalty was missed by Wycombe and Wimbledon levelled the tie again by scoring with theirs. The remaining kicks were converted and the tie was now 4-4; which meant that the match went to sudden death. The kicks went to 8-7 in Wycombe's favour and Wimbledon had to score to stay in the contest, but once again Martin Taylor was defiant and his save sent the Wanderers into round six. The epic match finally ended at 10-30pm leaving both players and supporters exhausted. Martin Taylor was named man of the match but in truth the whole team had performed heroically. It was certainly an evening of drama and high tension which had left me emotionally drained and the acquisition of an unforgettable memory.

In round six Wycombe had been drawn away to Premiership side Leicester City. At this latter part of the season Wycombe had now been beset by injuries and suspensions and were struggling to name a forward line especially with the Leicester game looming. At this point in time somebody in the Wycombe office, tongue in cheek suggested that the club put a request on the internet for a striker who was immediately available and not cup tied, so the message was sent. Surprisingly an answer came back from a Roy Essandoah who claimed that he met the criteria. Wycombe signed him and he played a couple of league games before the FA cup match.

I recall going by coach to Filbert Street, the home of Leicester, then sitting in the away stand waiting for the appearance of both teams. When the sides entered on to the pitch I noticed how big and imposing the Leicester players looked, unlike the smaller physiques of the Wycombe team. The game kicked off and Wycombe set about combatting the Leicester giants. As the game progressed Wycombe settled and managed to spring a few of their own attacks.

Wycombe in fact surprised their hosts by taking the lead and gradually gaining control. Leicester however remained a constant threat and with the lively Dean Sturridge, who in later years would play a prominent part in Wolves history was influential in a Leicester equalizer. As the game seemed to be heading for a draw, a further Wycombe attack resulted in a second and winning goal for the Wanderers. The goal scorer was Roy Essandoah, thus the fairy tale complete.

I was at the end where the triumphant goal was scored and it seemed for a moment that life had been put on freeze frame, as from start to finish when the ball was headed goal wards, gliding over the out stretched finger tips of the despairing Leicester goal keeper to the nestling in the back of the net, the operation seemed it had happened in slow motion, then came the realism of what it meant. The Wanderers had now reached the SEMI-FINALS of the FA CUP... and had been drawn to play Liverpool, the venue Villa Park.

Wycombe had some of their injured and suspended players back, but the comparison to the Liverpool team was like David and Goliath. When the Wycombe manager, Laurie Sanchez was asked how he was planning to beat Liverpool, he answered that he didn't have to, meaning that his side could hopefully get a draw and win the tie on penalties. Wycombe of course were meeting up again with their former manager Martin O'Neil who was now in charge of Aston Villa.

There was a good travelling away support to see the biggest FA cup match in Wycombe's history so far, and as every match in the earlier rounds had contained dramatic incident , could we dare expect more. The Wycombe fans were in good voice as the Wanderers set about trying to conquer their famous Premiership rivals. Meanwhile the Liverpool supporters were very apprehensive as their team faced an unknown opposition in Wycombe. The half time score was 0-0 and Wycombe had stuck to their task. It was only when Liverpool introduced Steven Gerard in the second half that the Wanderers were finally undone.

Wycombe were only fifteen minutes away from extra time but the skills of Gerard turned the tie Liverpool's way, a pin point cross from him found Heskey and Liverpool went 1-0 up. Another goal came quickly, this time from Fowler putting Liverpool 2-0 up and they now threatened to run amok. As with the matches in the earlier rounds of this season's competition Wycombe's desire and determination again re-surfaced and they weathered the Liverpool storm, in fact when Keith Ryan pulled a goal back 7 minutes from time Wycombe forced Liverpool on to the defensive for the rest of the match but couldn't break through again.

Wycombe's gallant cup run was over, final score Liverpool 2 Wycombe 1; but it had been an incredible journey. Also in this momentous season for Wycombe they were to create a new Guinness World record for the quickest time between two goals being scored, which now stands at 9 SECONDS. The match was in the football league, the date September 23rd 2000, played against Peterborough United. Wycombe won the match 2-0, the goals were scored by Jamie Bates and Jermaine McSporran either side of half time, a total time duration between both goals being scored 9 seconds. Into the naughties for Wolves and a season of total dis- belief best describes season 2001/2002. Wolves had assembled a good playing squad and had obvious intentions of having a serious crack at promotion. It seemed for most of the season that the campaign was on track, Wolves and Manchester City had pulled well clear of the rest of the field and it just seemed which one of them was going to be champions and who was going to be runners up. Unfortunately Wolves being Wolves decided to shoot themselves in both feet and from a position of strength their form slumped dramatically, wins became draws and draws became defeats.

Whilst they were crawling towards the finishing line West Brom of all teams were coming up fast on the outside lane and with seven wins from their last nine fixtures managed to overtake the Wanderers, finishing second and pushing the Wolves into third place. The Albion grabbed automatic promotion with 89 points and Wolves went into the play offs with 86 points. Wolves were 9 points clear of 4th place Millwall but had missed out badly due to inconsistent results the latter stages of the season.

Demoralised Wolves went into the play- off semi-finals where the opponents were Norwich City. Norwich had finished 6th in the league and played the first leg at their Carrow road ground. Wolves took the lead through Dean Sturridge but allowed Norwich back into the game, letting them score twice either side of half time. As the game went into injury time Norwich added a third and thus took a 3-1 lead to the second leg at Molineux. In the second leg Wolves bombarded the Norwich defence but could only manage a 1-0 win which meant that Norwich went through 3-2 on aggregate.

Further Into the second millennium and a special time for me, both personally and my supporting of the Wanderers. Wolves having now spent several seasons in the second tier of the football league, currently called the Championship had the chance in season 2002/2003 to return to the top flight via the play offs. Having finished in 6th position in the Championship Wolves played and defeated Reading 3-1 in a two legged semi-final, this result against Reading was particularly pleasing as earlier in that season we had lost at home to them in the league.

I remember on the drive home after the league defeat to show that we weren't downhearted we had our Wolves flags flying out of the car window. Unfortunately as we had similar journeys home we were passed by a car full of Reading fans, who when seeing our car and flags started cheering and laughing. We shouted back "it's a long way to go yet". Sure enough when we played Reading again in the league at their ground towards the end of the season we beat them 1-0 and this result helped get us into the play offs.

The final was played in Cardiff against Sheffield United and this was the Wanderers first appearance in a play-off final. Sheffield United were managed by Neil Warnock who was a past master at getting teams promoted and as Wolves had only previously drawn and lost their league fixtures with them that season, started the match as underdogs. I and friend Simon had got our Play off Final tickets and decided that we would travel to Cardiff by train.

Our journey would mean driving from home in High Wycombe and catching the train at READING railway station, we just had to give those Wolves car flags another airing to make sure if any Reading fans were about they knew who was in the final. When we got to Cardiff, the atmosphere in the Millennium stadium was electrifying as the final got under way. Wolves found a passion and determination that overwhelmed their rivals and their bold and attacking play earned them a 3-0 half time lead. At the start of the second half Sheffield United who had been blown away in the first half came out with a more aggressive attitude and set about attempting to reduce the arrears.

In the first minute of the re-start Sheffield United were awarded a penalty but Matt Murray in the Wolves goal was equal to it and the 3-0 score remained intact.

The Blades from Sheffield knew it wasn't going to be their day when they struck a Wolves post mid-way through the second half and the game was concluded without any further scoring. The Wolves were back in the top division and would play 2003/2004 in the Premier League. The euphoria of competing in the Premier League was however soon dampened by the poor opening results.

The first game saw the Wanderers crash 5-1 at Blackburn and the opening home fixture fared no better as Charlton inflicted a 4-0 defeat. It was quickly apparent that the Wolves squad was not strong enough for the demands of premiership football. Despite a few good results including a 1-0 home win against champions elect Manchester United, the bad start ensured that the Wolves remained in the lower section of the table all season and that relegation was the likely outcome.

The other notable performance of the season was the home fixture against Leicester, trailing 0-3 at half time the Wanderers over turned this deficit to win 4-3, a remarkable come back and high drama. Those fans that had given up and left early missed one of the best Premier League turn arounds ever. My passion for the Wanderers will never wain but my greatest love will always be the love that I have for my partner and soul mate Linda. When she agreed to be my wife I was overjoyed and we set out to plan our wedding day. Now of course Linda knew of my love for the Wanderers and wasn't surprised when I suggested that we got married at the Molineux Stadium, but I was taken aback when she agreed.

We fixed our date for Fri April 30th 2004; the ceremony was to be conducted at Sir Jack's suite in the Billy Wright stand. Sir Jack even sent us a telegram message wishing us well for our pending marriage. We had arranged for our families and friends to be transported from High Wycombe to Wolverhampton by coach. On the Saturday we hired a box for our wedding party to watch the Wolves v Everton fixture with us. In the Everton team that day was a young Wayne Rooney and despite going a goal down Wolves fought back to win 2-1. A great result for our wedding weekend but unfortunately this win was one of only seven and after just one season the Wolves again were relegated back to the Championship.

The memories of that weekend will be with me forever, marrying the best lady in the world in the home stadium of the best football club in the world, can't be bad. The return to the championship brought with it a fresh challenge; having experienced the premiership it was important that the club returned to the top flight as soon as possible and the 2008/2009 did in fact see the Wolves return as champions under the guidance of Mick McCarthy. This time around the team adapted more quickly and a more positive campaign ensured that the Wanderers season lasted the distance. Going into the final stages Wolves needed to pick up vital points from three crucial away games played within a week. The games were Burnley, Aston Villa and West Ham and I remember that week as VINTAGE CLARET because all three oppositions played in claret and blue and Wolves obtained two wins and a draw against them thus securing a second consecutive season in the Premiership. Wycombe had now firmly established as a league side and in 2011 had achieved the 3rd tier of the Football League.

CHAPTER NINE

THE CHANGES

I have over the years enjoyed my football watching and because like many fans I had started my supporting as boy and continuing into my adulthood I have witnessed and had many memorable experiences. From my early years in the sixties, to the present times in the second millennium I have seen many significant changes both in the social and sporting world. These changes have had major bearings how football clubs have had to adapt and in particular to the clubs that I follow Wolves and Wycombe. A lot of football stadiums in the early years were built close to the communities that wanted to go to the matches, including sites in the town and city centres. This was fine at the time but as populations and industry grew it later put pressure and financial demands on the clubs, forcing them to reconsider their locations as the ground they were situated on was now much sought after. Wycombe finally moved from the Loakes Park ground after 95 years of residence thus allowing the neighbouring hospital to expand and the club re-established a couple of miles away at the Adams Park ground. The gates from Loakes Park have been incorporated at the new stadium. Wolves were taken over in the eighties by property developers the Bhatti brothers who only wanted the ground and had no interest in the football club; luckily the club was wrestled from their clutches before it faced extinction. On the political front in the early seventies when the country was held to ransom by the trade unions we had the three day working week, which meant that the country had to be more fugal with its fuel and energy supplies. The television network would close down at 10-30pm each night to reduce the use of electricity and evening football matches requiring floodlights were curtailed; most were re-scheduled for the afternoons.

CHAPTER TEN

THE FIRST 45 YEARS

To conclude, at the end of my FIRST 45 years of watching the Wanderers both clubs have left me with lasting memories and it has been a fantastic journey so far, with the highs of promotions and the lows of relegations with the odd cup final thrown in. As I end this current chapter both clubs have forged a unique but unwanted double for me, i.e. RELEGATION from their respective leagues in the same year; at the end of season 2011/2012 Wycombe occupied 21st position in division one and returned to the second division of the football league and Wolves finished bottom of the Premiership thus bringing an end to their Premier status after three consecutive seasons in the top flight.

This was particularly frustrating as the previous season produced notable home victories against both Manchester clubs and Chelsea together with an excellent away win at Liverpool. The 2011/2012 campaign had started well with two wins and a draw from the opening three matches and the Wolves had TWICE topped the league. Unfortunately some inconsistent performances and the inability to keep a clean sheet was to prove costly and the Wanderers rapidly slid down the table. Certain sections of the crowd had started to call for the resignation of manager Mick McCarthy as the team took residence in the bottom section of the table. Despite receiving the dreaded vote of confidence from Chairman Steve Morgan the dismal home performance against arch rivals West Brom was to be instrumental and the original decision to keep faith with manager McCarthy was overturned and he was sacked after the 1-5 home defeat. There then followed the farcical situation when the manager who was lined up to replace McCarthy turned the club down and with the need to get results quickly if the Wolves were to get enough points to avoid the drop,had made the situation desperate.

To add to the bungled handling of the McCarthy sacking Wolves then failed to find a Manager to see out the last dozen crucial league games. In desperation the club appointed Terry Connor who had been at Wolves for the last 12 years serving under 4 managers as coach and had been assistant manager to Mick McCarthy at the time of his dismissal. The effort started well for Connor gaining a vital 2-2 away draw at high flying Newcastle coming back from 2-0 down but the problems that had been there all season were still there and without fresh ideas it proved more of the same was being served up. Connor failed to get a win in his short time as manager and Wolves finished bottom and relegated. He left the post with a management record of played 13 won 0 drew 4 lost 9 and on reflection was McCarthy's termination badly timed? Wycombe had a similar season some good results in particular the 1-0 home win against Sheffield United but also lacked consistency together with some woeful performances suffered the same fate as Wolves.

Certainly following a club like Wolves or Wycombe, always allows for optimism even though the expectations are limited but the satisfactions out way the frustrations and disappointments. A win or good result is treasured which I'm sure is often wasted on supporters of the so called bigger clubs where success is taken for granted or demanded. Now in my fifties I still look forward to every match that I can attend following the Wanderers.

Appendix

Having seen quite a few teams and players over the years I have often been asked, what would be my all-time favourite Wycombe and Wolves teams? Obviously everyone has their own views but these are mine based on players that I've actually seen play.

WYCOMBE 4-4-2
1.John Maskell GK, 2.Paul Birdseye RB, 3.Roger Grant LB, 4. Noel Ashford MF, 5.John Delaney CH, 6.Glyn Creaser CH, 7.Dave Carroll F, 8.Larry Pritchard MF, 9.Keith Searle F, 10.Tony Horseman F, 11.Steve Guppy F. SUBS Martin Taylor GK, Mark West, Micky Holifield, Keith Scott, Keith Ryan.

WOLVES 4-4-2
1.Mike Stowell GK, 2.Derek Parkin RB, 3.Bobby Thompson LB, 4.Mike Bailey MF, 5.Joleon Lescott CH, 6.Frank Munro CH, 7.Robbie Keane F, 8.Ken Hibbitt MF, 9.Steve Bull F, 10.John Richards F, 11.Dave Wagstaffe F, SUBS Wayne Hennessey GK, Derek Dougan, Willie Carr, Matt Jarvis, Hugh Curran.

My favourite Wycombe player of all time has to be Larry Pritchard, although he came to the club late in his career his experience and energy proved invaluable to the Wanderers. His style of play reminded me of the Manchester City and England player Colin Bell. My favourite Wolves player remains the legendary Steve Bull who typified what I expect to see as a fan. Bully has smashed all the club scoring records at Wolves since being rescued from the stripy lot from down the road. His loyalty to Wolves has been without question especially when the bigger clubs came a calling. I remember the 89/90 league cup tie 2nd leg against Aston Villa which was played at the Molineux. Wolves were trailing by a goal to nil when Bully equalised just before half time but in doing so he collided with the Villa keeper and was knocked unconscious. It looked bad when Steve was stretchered off; the half time talk was of how long would he be out of action for, a week month? We shouldn't have worried the man took his place for the SECOND HALF.